The Burning

ANNA SELBY grew up in Shropshire, she worked abroad before moving to Norwich to study English Literature and do a Creative Writing Masters at the University of East Anglia. Her poems have been published in various publications, including *Magma*, *The Rialto* and *Smiths Knoll* and her poetry–dance collaborations have been shortlisted for The Oxford Samuel Beckett Theatre Trust Award, featured on the BBC Culture Show and tour nationally. Her poems often explore our connection with water and are influenced by poetry from Eastern Europe. In 2012, she organised Poetry Parnassus festival and co–edited *The World Record* anthology (Bloodaxe). She lives in London and works as Literature and Spoken Word Programmer at the Southbank Centre.

I0087987

The Burning

by

ANNA SELBY

SALT

CROMER

PUBLISHED BY SALT PUBLISHING
12 Norwich Road, Cromer, Norfolk NR27 0AX, United Kingdom

© Anna Selby, 2013

The right of Anna Selby to be identified as the
author of this work has been asserted by her in accordance
with Section 77 of the Copyright, Designs and Patents Act 1988.

Salt Publishing 2013

Printed and bound in the United Kingdom by Lightning Source UK Ltd

Typeset in Swift 9.5 / 13

ISBN 978 1 84471 951 8 pamphlet

1 3 5 7 9 8 6 4 2

To my family

Contents

Acknowledgements

Grateful thanks to family, friends and colleagues who helped with this pamphlet; to my tutors; Salt and the editors of the following publications where some of these poems appeared: *The Caravan*, *Magma*, *Missing Slate Magazine*, *Poems in Which*, *The Rialto*, *Smiths Knoll* and *Ghost of Gone Birds* anthology, published by Bloomsbury.

Choreographer, Heather Eddington, commissioned several of the poems, including versions of *Washing My Father* and *The Death of the Fish March*.

Thank you also to Aldeburgh South Lookout, Cove Park, Robert and Sian Petty, Patricia and David Stevens for time and space to write.

The Burning

The First Time I Saw Your Winter

When I rebranded snowdrops
they turned into shame lilies;
juniper berries were Nordic furies,
leaves, luns: from the Old
meaning to let a breath
flee from idleness.

Your language
got more picasz, less hefda, more
shenğikï. Each word became a wire
birds sprang from.

Your turn now.
Shoo. Stand in front of a mirror
not knowing you've been named.
It will be as if, for the first time ever,
you've just seen yourself.

The Second Dance

after James Cousins' duet, There We Have Been

I will lay my body on your body one day.
When I lay my body on your body it will be flat.
I will peel us together from the toes:
pack my calves onto your shins,
float your knees into my knees.
I will sit on you, an incongruous hound.
Neither of our bodies will be clothed.
It will be deep winter. Our bodies
lit like opera singers
on a floor in a small wooden hut
hours from the nearest city, its name
crammed with Xs and Qs we write on paper,
because when we say it
we feel inadequate. We will be realising
we don't love each other,
but we haven't told out bodies
and our hands have made a spitting fire
the buds of our knuckles unfold to.
Will we regret then this monster we've made
or love again the strangeness of our shape –
our shadow flooding the ceiling, laughter
scuttling up into the woods like raucous bugs?

Where I Come From

Where I come from
people don't look at you
the same way if you leave.

Where I come from
three generations are knitted for
in the same bed.

Where I come from
they look the same: six siblings
washed in the same sink.

Where I come from
your surname is
Grittith, Shuker, Beddows.

Where I come from
you must watch your head
on the stairs.

Where I come from
they don't look at you the same way
as you look at them.

Where I come from
you watch and you listen
and say little, little, little.

Dunwich Burning

'The burning' is a phrase used in north Norfolk to describe phosphorescence

My accomplice stumbles away out of colour,
then stops at the edge abruptly, as if the sea
were a window that appeared in his house.
The ship–like buildings of midnight mount behind us:
moonset fugitives, two smugglers wading into our silence.
We swim above a town they say sunk beneath us.
If the tide were low enough, the wind
would rush through the bell towers. I turn back,
skin crackling and could cry or sing,
shaking constellations from my hands. Stars slip
off my fingers, like scales from a fisherwoman's knife.
We lay each other out in wet sand.
The waves extinguish themselves,
tug and resist bare feet, bare shins, bare skin.
And yes, the town might never have existed,
but even if you imagine it, it will lie
somewhere there before you. The legend
is still hauled from the depths, and there are hours
of fire left, and the sea is sinking in.

The Early Shift

Tell me again
about your friend's uncle:
the pilferer, poacher –
how he waited all night for you
in camouflage, shotgun cocked
over one arm, morning papers
bundled at his feet.

How he said,
I'm here to protect you,
fumbled in his jacket,
pulled out a dead rabbit
dangled like a prize won at a fair:
wet, limp, legs tied and black eyes
stumped with questions.
You'd never been so close
to a gun before.

Washing My Father

after Doina Ioanid

Sadness moved into my house.
It whispered in the corner
until I stopped watching it.
When it tired, it spoke out from the dark.
Its voice was sisterly.

How long will you stay here? I asked.
But sadness only speaks when it wants to.
When its whim spins and points you
in a new direction.

When I turn back,
the oranges are black in the bowl.
I hold my father's jaw.
His tremor ratchets through me.

Why do you lift your father like a drowned man? Sadness asks.
Huge waves are breaking over the burnt–out pier.

Death of the Fish March

White birds know which leader to follow,
how to fake it, how to roll and whip their wings daily,
a reincarnated chorus: wailers flailing
behind the pyre. Gulls flipping themselves over with grief,
a flurry of grief, grief the slow motoring
chug, grief the car kept ticking, grief shoving
grief out of the way for a glimpse, grief the white handkerchiefs
waving them off, grief the paper blown from a burnt–out building,
grief the cold hand on your neck, grief
a flung back beak, grief the shriek
as they pass over, grief the loss as they move out of shot,
grief circling above as they get closer to the handing over of the dead,
always close enough to feel the breath rise
from the trawler, the last heat of the boat,
the shine of death as the offerings slip from the nets.
My grief wonders what my grandfather whistled,
what tune it was that made my grandmother follow.
Death does not wait for fisherwomen, they tug it to them
gasping, and stay with it until the end,
scrubbing the dead from their fingernails.
Only when they return with the bodies glinting,
can the procession begin again.

Swimming in the Abandoned Quarry

It's like dying, you shout,
then leap
hot out of your own life.

But such a short death:
your feet barely down
before your head crowns,

so the pool seems confused:
a blue–skinned creature
trembling at its own dream.

When we dive,
we dive with our hands
and legs bound –

dead meat
hung upside down.
The water wakes.

Watch it choke.
Feel a beast–heart bloat,
swell,

then settle,
like a parachute
in the night trees.

Is it Too Late for the Bath

given that all the car doors
have shut and the last foot rang
the drain cover – our gong –
and the foxes

>imitating dogs
>are lapping the dark tennis court,
>where only leaves dry as rice
>roll over the sidelines

and back across
in a slumbering waltz?
We are no use if we can't see
the boundaries' white marks.

>Given this, and the ominous
>shapes anointing the sink,
>it is too late to turn the tap
>East in a shared house

where the old Estonian sleeps,
and the heavy German
wakes at the flinch
of a match.

An Intimate Dinner with Raised Voices

This house is spoilt. It overreacts. Repeats every step back
as a flapmouthed, bumfed–up cuss. The front gate smacks
a warning shot, then every door is a thug after.
At dinner, when you turn to the fool next to you and whisper,
I'd merely like to suggest – you make an address,
all hollering at each other in the same room, loud enough
for the drunk–klutz bashing down the alley to listen to.
Even the washing up is a scrum in a dock: plates clashing
however gently you place them one on top of the other.
No matter how high up the house you climb, their laughter
tracks you, shrill as a Gatling gun and the chairs drag
under the table as they do at the end of a lesson. In bed,
even your bones are stirred to speak, listening all night
to the rain drip and tunnel your ribs with measly fists.

The Lost Art of Disappearing

after The Swimmer, *by John Cheever*

An ex goes under at Waterloo,
comes up, years later,
on a rooftop bar in Soho.
Everywhere has its disappearances:
the front of a cliff house slices off,
clean, quick, like a mask plucked;

towns drowned below reservoirs
sit still as dioramas. At night,
from Primrose Hill, you see parks vanish
into black canyons, shop doorways,
where homeless men flicker in
and out of the dark.

Moving to a city is its own trick. Watch me:
the old falling–through–a–trapdoor trick,
the old stepping–off–a–roof–onto–a–roof trick.
You see the greystone years ahead of you,
the greystone years behind you,
skyscrapers lost in low cloud,

so your toes curl up, feet tilt
to glimpse the top. Any moment,
a man can fall, all the workers
look up, a circus act: hands
stretched out, heads tilted back,
readying themselves for the catch.

Recipes for Quiet Sons

You come home with puzzles in you
bound tight as artichoke hearts.
I find them on the wrong shelf,
hook them out of glass jars and leave them
spoiling the worktop like a poor day's catch.

Today, you walked in an old wood,
saw how rain clamps fir cones shut.
That's all you'll tell me.
Easing your coat off with wet fingers,
I slow cook your riddles with rosemary,
allow the first breath to steam our throats.

Your fists loosen: lotuses opening.

The Many Reasons

I was high when the drunk
forgot his vows, high
when we risked
our bodies on the balcony,
high when the Actuary asked,
Did I – ? High when the Russian
wrote out the many reasons why
I should keep on trying
to love him.

Behind me,
there were rows of people
who wouldn't have wavered,
so *yes* I kept saying, *yes, yes.*
Yes struck the wall
until I believed it existed,
my vowel sighs like smoke rings
and O° the open window,
blinds tigering glass skin.

How Sundays Would Sound if
People Described Them

A fly dies on a windowsill. It rains
a lot in a small town. A man thinks he's seen
his dead father in the shed again. The crux is
there's a fox in the garden, where there's never
been one before. Someone has a rambunctious dream.
Sussex horticultural show – nobody knows who's won.
A girl runs through a wood, wet, then sits. A couple
have sex on the worktop, it's the last time, afterwards
they discover there isn't enough bread. A man
summarises a year's Sundays, as if they were
lift–pitches for uncommissioned films.

52 Versions of Hope
after A Game of Patience, *by Meredith Frampton*

It was a trick he taught you well:
how to show only one card while you
turn, move through the circle dealt,
the fan you're surrounded with: face up,
high, a queen giving nothing away.

You pin your hand over the other
not ready to see what you'll lay
because the one you keep hidden
could be revealed with a wristflick
and that would be the end of it,
the end of staring at high white walls.

My mother's mother,
who stands no matter who knocks.
Put down your card and lift the other,
or I'll find you fifty years later, folded
over a low table, that same card
held out like a compact before you.

Timelapse

An easy mistake: just a wink of a doubt
that you were the one pin–pricked and slumbering,
that it was a new term overnight.

You look away, and in the time it takes to whistle,
the old orchard mocks into white,
the lane gets a green mohican.

When you put your feet into a county of thistles
they duplicate with each blink. When you squint
at the rape field, yellow spreads like brashfire.

You rub your eyes and suddenly a solar system
of dandelions pounce, orbit the house.
Your youngest is pregnant.

It is the finale trick: the multiplying rabbits
hiccoughing in and out of a hat,
vanishing flocks, geese reappearing,

each time in a different spot.
You should lie down now. Have a power nap.
It will be autumn next time you wake.

Duck Eggs and Keats Instead of Grace

Why can't it always be like this?

Opening the door of a car
left in sunshine.

Eating olives at night and arguing
about apostrophes.

Leaving in the dark hours
of the morning.

Reciting Keats, instead of grace
over omelettes.

Finishing your glass,
and finding it full

and finding it full again,
and finding it full.